The World's Deadliest

The Deadliest Weather
on Earth

by Connie Colwell Miller

Reading Consultant:
Barbara J. Fox
Reading Specialist
North Carolina State University

Content Consultant:
Joseph M. Moran, PhD
Associate Director of Education
American Meteorological Society
Washington, D.C.

CAPSTONE PRESS
a capstone imprint

Blazers is published by Capstone Press,
151 Good Counsel Drive, P.O. Box 669, Mankato, Minnesota 56002.
www.capstonepress.com

092009
005619WZS10

Library of Congress Cataloging-in-Publication Data
Miller, Connie Colwell, 1976–
    The deadliest weather on Earth / by Connie Colwell Miller.
    p. cm. — (Blazers. The world's deadliest)
    Summary: "Describes deadly weather and what makes it dangerous" — Provided by publisher.
    Includes bibliographical references and index.
    ISBN 978-1-4296-3934-7 (lib. bdg.)
    1. Climatic extremes — Juvenile literature. I. Title.
QC981.8.C53M55 2010
551.6 — dc22   2009026655

Editorial Credits
Christopher L. Harbo, editor; Matt Bruning, designer; Svetlana Zhurkin, media researcher;
    Laura Manthe, production specialist

Photo Credits
Alamy/A. T. Willett, 13; Icelandic Photo Agency, 17; Jon Arnold Images, 21; Mark Romesser, 11;
    Royal Geographical Society, 7
Getty Images/Absodels, 29; Reportage/Mike Goldwater, 15; Riser/Angelo Cavalli, 25; Stone/Alan
    R. Moller, cover, 23; Stone/Charles Doswell III, 5
NASA, 27
Shutterstock/Jhaz Photography, 19; Samuel Acosta, 9

TABLE OF CONTENTS

DEADLY WEATHER

Mother Nature has a mean streak. Every year, thousands of people around the world die in severe weather. Get ready to learn about the deadliest weather on the planet!

SORT OF DANGEROUS

THAT BITES!

Freezing temperatures are icy killers. Low air temperatures and strong winds can cause **frostbite**. A drop in body temperature can cause deadly hypothermia.

frostbite – a condition that occurs when cold temperatures freeze skin

DEADLY FACT

Hypothermia happens when your body temperature drops below 95 degrees Fahrenheit (35 degrees Celsius).

BLOWING WINDS

Powerful winds whip up dust and sand into wicked storms. Strong winds knock down trees. Falling trees strike cars, houses, and people. Windblown dust and sand cause breathing problems that can lead to death.

DEADLY FACT

In 1999, severe winds blew down millions of trees in northern Minnesota. Sixty people in the area were hurt by falling trees.

HAIL!

Frozen chunks of ice called hail sometimes fall during thunderstorms. Small hail damages cars, homes, and crops. Large hail can injure or kill people and animals. Some hailstones are as large as baseballs!

DEADLY FACT

Hail can fall at more than 100 miles (161 kilometers) per hour!

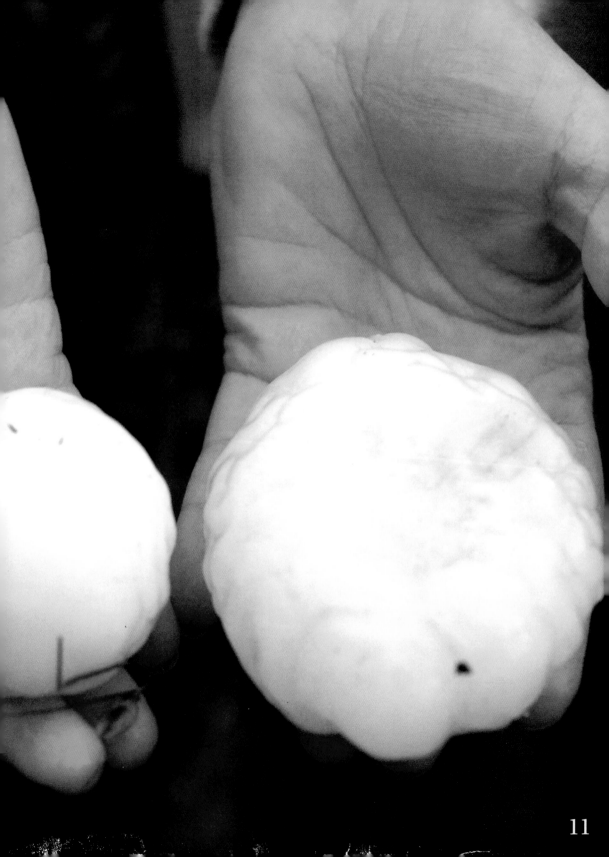

UNDERWATER

Heavy rains in a short time can cause flash floods. Rising water quickly sweeps cars off roads and covers homes. Floods kill more than 70 people in the United States each year.

DEADLY FACT

During flooding, waste matter mixes with drinking water. This dirty mixture causes illness to spread quickly through cities.

Chapter 3

VERY DANGEROUS

DRIED UP!

Long periods of dry weather may not seem deadly. But **droughts** cause crops to wither and die. Without food, animals and people starve to death.

drought – a long period of weather with little or no rainfall

DEADLY FACT

Between the 1960s and 1980s, droughts in Africa killed more than 100,000 people.

WHITEOUT

Blizzards bring whirling snow and icy winds. Travelers get lost in **whiteouts** that make surroundings hard to see. Icy roads cause deadly traffic accidents.

DEADLY FACT

Many people die of heart attacks while shoveling heavy snow.

whiteout – a blizzard condition that makes objects hard to see

STRUCK DOWN!

Thunderstorms can have deadly lightning. Lightning strikes **electrocute** people. Even a nearby strike is hot enough to burn a person.

electrocute – to kill with a severe electric shock

EXTREME RAIN

Monsoons bring much-needed rain to Asia and Africa. But they can also cause deadly floods. These floods destroy homes and crops. People drown in floodwaters.

DEADLY FACT

On March 10, 2009, a monsoon hit Bombay, India. The storm dumped 37 inches (94 centimeters) of rain on the city.

monsoon – a seasonally changing wind that causes wet summers and dry winters

Chapter 4

EXTREMELY DANGEROUS

DANGER
Meter

TWISTERS

Tornadoes destroy whatever they touch. These windstorms spin as fast as 300 miles (483 kilometers) per hour. Strong tornadoes are powerful enough to suck up people, cars, and buildings.

DEADLY *FACT*

In 1925, a deadly tornado traveled from Missouri to Indiana. It killed almost 700 people.

DEADLY HURRICANES

Hurricanes pound coastlines with powerful winds and sheets of rain. Their **storm surges** flood low-lying coastal areas. People caught in a storm surge get swept away and drown.

DEADLY *FACT*

The Great Galveston Hurricane of 1900 killed 8,000 people. Most of the dead drowned in the storm surge.

storm surge – a sudden, strong rush of water that happens as a hurricane moves onto land

TROPICAL DISASTERS

Typhoons and cyclones are the same as hurricanes. Typhoons rip through the North Pacific. Cyclones strike the South Pacific. Both types of storms kill thousands of people each year.

DEADLY FACT

In 2003, Typhoon Rusa killed 213 people in South Korea.

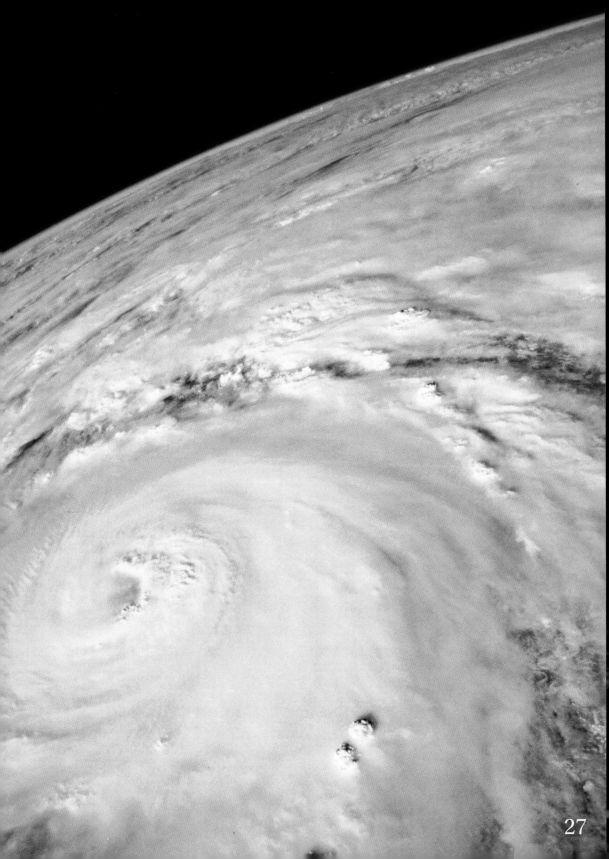

HOT SEAT

Heat waves kill more people each year than any other type of weather. Extremely high temperatures and high humidity can cause **heatstroke**. Whether it's heavy rain or strong winds, weather can turn deadly in an instant!

DEADLY FACT

In 1996, California's Death Valley topped 120 degrees Fahrenheit (49 degrees Celsius) on 40 days.

heatstroke – collapse caused by working too long in very hot conditions

GLOSSARY

drought (DROUT) — a long period of weather with little or no rainfall

electrocute (i-LEK-truh-kyoot) — to be killed with a severe electric shock

frostbite (FRAWST-byt) — a condition that occurs when cold temperatures freeze skin

heatstroke (HEET STROHK) — collapse caused by working too long in very hot conditions

hypothermia (hye-puh-THUR-mee-uh) — a life-threatening condition that can occur when a person's body temperature drops several degrees below normal

monsoon (mon-SOON) — a seasonally changing wind that causes wet summers and dry winters

storm surge (STORM SURJ) — a sudden, strong rush of water that happens as a hurricane moves onto land

whiteout (WITE-out) — a blizzard condition that makes objects hard to see

READ MORE

Farndon, John. *Extreme Weather.* Experience. New York: DK, 2007.

Marsico, Katie. *Wild Weather Days.* Scholastic News Nonfiction Readers. New York: Children's Press, 2007.

Sengupta, Monalisa. *Wild Weather.* Wild Nature. New York: PowerKids Press, 2008.

INTERNET SITES

FactHound offers a safe, fun way to find Internet sites related to this book. All of the sites on FactHound have been researched by our staff.

Here's all you do:

Visit *www.facthound.com*

FactHound will fetch the best sites for you!

INDEX